The Changing Global Marketplace Landscape

The Changing Global Marketplace Landscape

Understanding Customer Intentions, Attitudes, Beliefs, and Feelings

Bob Ssekyanzi

Print information available on the last page.

Rev. date: 04/04/2016

To order additional copies of this book, contact:
Xlibris
1-888-795-4274
www.Xlibris.com
Orders@Xlibris.com
739367

CONTENTS

To My Wife, Anna: Thank you very much for the everlasting love, encouragement, and support in everything.

To our Children, Brenda, Rehema, Bob Jr., & Penny: Thank you very much for being a reflection of God's love and endurance.

To our Grandchildren, Denzel and Dee: We love you dearly.

To my late parents, John & Philly: Thank you very much for everything you taught me.

May your Souls Rest In Peace.

Customer service started out as help offered at a desk at the back of a department store, and evolved with the invention of the telephone. In today's hyper-connected world, and given the competitive environment in the global marketplace, customer service is more than just the helpdesk associate who answers your questions when you call an 800 number for help. It has revolved and grown to encompass every interaction that a customer has with a brand. It includes phone, email, chat, web forms, and social communications, as well as self-service support sites. And it happens before, during, and after a sale

When it comes to defining the logistical concept of customer service, not everyone agrees on what it is exactly that makes up good customer service, but bad customer service isn't quite as hard to define, because while specific service standards vary based on your company, industry and expectations, you can bet that customers will recognize bad customer service when it happens to them. Perhaps most important of all is to is recognize that good customer service encompasses any interaction, online or off, that a consumer or potential customer may have with your company, and it includes the entire experience, from initial contact to final sale and beyond.

Perhaps most important of all is to recognize that good customer service encompasses any interaction, online or offline, that a consumer or potential customer may have with your company, and it includes the entire experience, from initial contact to final sale and beyond. In a nutshell, we can summarize the logistical components of customer service as the act of taking care of the customers' needs by providing and delivering professional, helpful, high quality service and assistance before, during, and after the customers' requirements are met.

As the competition in the global marketplace continues to change, companies are faced with the challenge of re-evaluating the way they approach and deal with customer service issues. One of the questions asked on a daily basis is: **What exactly is customer service?**

Quality customer service entails providing efficient, quick and friendly service, building strong relationships with customers, handling complaints quickly and responding to customers' issues on time. Quality customer service is the best way to keep customers coming back, thus ensuring long-term success.

Customers hold opinions about services, products, stores, advertising, salespeople, shopping, other customers, spending, and the list never ends. To a large extent, some of the opinions represent what we like and dislike. Other opinions stand for what we as a community believe and how we feel. Still, other customer opinions reflect the judgments about how we intend to behave in the future. We live in an environment that is continuously changing and is driven by a gazillion of many facets of issues. As the landscape in the global marketplace continues to change, companies from small to large, are on a daily basis of operation, confronted with the challenge of forecasting customer behavior by asking them what they intend to do. The main focus is to understand the customer intentions which can accurately predict the future behavior toward the products and services being offered.

As the competition in the global marketplace continues to heat up, companies-small and large are challenged to have the most skilled staff with the ability to predict how people will act as customers toward the products and services being offered. Companies often lose money because they underestimate or overestimate the issues pertaining to demand. Beyond what customers buy, companies are interested in predicting where they will buy, when they will buy, and how much they will buy. This interest goes beyond buying. Customer service departments of every organization must determine the logistical component of associates needed to handle issues pertaining to customer service; such as inquiries and product, and service complaints. Such determinations must be based on estimates of the number of customers that require daily attention.

Customer Intentions

In all ways, it is by no accident that one of the greatest and important skills any organization possess is the ability to predict how people act as customers of the intended services and products put on the market for them to buy. Beyond what customers buy, companies are additionally interested in predicting where they will buy, when they will buy, and how much they will buy. This interest in customer intentions goes beyond just buying products and services.

So, based on that perspective, how can companies predict what the product and service consumers will do? The basic answer to this may be to rely on the past behavior in order to forecast what may happen in the future. If the customers have bought the same brand of a product for a measurable amount of time, it may be safe to anticipate that the same customer segment will buy the same brand of products and services during their next trip to the store or location where the product and/or service is located. But things change, and what happened in the past may not reflect what may become far less relevant than what is happening in today's ever changing market landscape.

As the trend in the global marketplace continues to change unpredictably, an alternative approach to predicting customer behavior takes on a new degree of uncertainty, and may involve asking customers what their intentions are. Customer intentions are subjective judgments about the behaviors toward services and product will be in the future. As a result, there are many types of customer intentions such as: **(a) Purchase intentions:** These are intentions aim at what products and/or services will buy in the future. **(b) Shopping intentions:** These intentions aim at where companies plan on making products and/or services available for purchases. **(c) Spending intentions:** These intentions aim at finding out how much money customers will spend on products and/or services. **(d) Search intentions:** These intentions aim at engaging in external search about the advantages and disadvantages of buying any given product and/or service. (e) Consumption intentions: These intentions aim at the degree of engagement in a particular consumption activity (e.g., watching a Television exercise, or sports event, etc.,)

We live in an environment where things continue to change on a daily basis. Customer intentions toward a particular product and/or service can likewise change. Unanticipated circumstances can cause many things to change. Despite the gazillion of limitations we face as people in our everyday encounters with our business lives, customers' intentions may still be one of the company's best bet for predicting the future behavior toward products and/or services. When Quaker State tested the potential of a new engine treatment product, purchase intentions were a key factor in forecasting future demand for the product. "You can project that data into future market share and trial usage," says Bob Cohen, former executive vice president of the innovations center at Quaker State. "It is the best information you can have to evaluate whether or not to go forward and invest more money."

Although it is never an easy task to control how customers act upon their intentions, there are other ways to control or at least be aware of the will that influence intentions' predictive accuracy. It is very important that companies pay more focus on the concept of intentions measurement. Intention measures should fully correspond to the to-be-predicted customer behavior. If a company wants to predict whether customers will buy its products and/or services at a particular time, then the intention measures should specify this (e.g., "Do you intend to buy milk next time you go to the grocery store?"). As the correspondence between the intention measures and the to-be-predicted behavior becomes weaker, so does the intention's predictive power. Measuring what customers intend to do may sometimes be less predictive of their future behavior than measuring what they expect to do. If you ask Alcohol consumers whether they intend to stop drinking alcohol, many will answer with a resounding "no!" Yet fulfilling these intentions is not an easy exercise. Most times habit is more powerful than willpower. A more realistic assessment might be obtained by measuring behavioral expectations. Behavioral expectations aim at capturing the perceived likelihood of performing a behavior. Although alcohol drinkers may hold very strong intentions to not quit, they may report more moderate expectations of doing so because of past popularity.

The existence of uncontrollable factors interferes with the ability to do what companies in the first place intend to do in order to keep pace with the competition in the global marketplace. As the competition in the global marketplace continues to challenge organizations, it turns out that customer intentions are helpful as an indicator of the possible effects of certain marketing activities.

Similarly, think of a company trying to implement a significant change in its products and/or services because of the belief that by so doing, sales will greatly increase. Nonetheless, the company recognizes that the purported change may not work and might even impact the company's sales. Before actually implementing any given change, the company needs to explore whether the change influences the customers' intentions in the desired direction. Customer intentions may also provide an informative indication of a company's likely success in retaining customers.

Customer Attitudes

A favorable attitude toward a product is an essential prerequisite in order for customers to have a favorable purchase or consumption intention. If customers don't like a certain product and/or service, they can take their business elsewhere. A customer may like one brand but intend to buy another brand that is liked even more. The basic point here is that having a favorable attitude toward a product and/or service is different from having a favorable attitude toward buying or consuming the product. Product attitudes represent a certain portion of the attitudes which influence customer behavior. It is to this point, it is very important to understand that attitudes toward other types of brand associations form a bigger portion of consumer attitudes. Attitudes play an important part in determining an organization's advertising effectiveness. Attitudes toward the advertising have been shown repeatedly to act as a significant determinant of the product/service attitudes held after viewing the advertisement.

Attitude Formation

Suppose sometime last year while watching a football game on TV you saw a commercial for a new car that took your attention. You gave extra attention to the commercial, much more than you usual. You carefully processed the information presented in the commercial about the car's attributes. You became even more interested in the car. You made the mental note to yourself to drive that car the next time when the opportunity comes. In this example, we see that an attitude toward the car was formed. Admittedly, this attitude is held rather tentatively. At this point, all needed to go on is the commercial, not always the most reliable source of information. Note that this attitude toward the car was based on those beliefs formed about the car. Your beliefs about the car's logistical components and location led you to conclude that it was the type of car that you would like to own.

Attitudes are not carved in stone. As the competitive environment in the global marketplace continue to challenge companies, today's craze may easily become tomorrow's has-been, as clothing and toy manufacturers know all too well. Changing customer attitudes is a frequent business objective. Often, however, attitudes toward products/services change because of encountering something which warrants revision. Attitude persistence represents an attitude's immunity to corrosion. The attitude held prior to consumption would bear little resemblance to the attitude held after consumption of the product/service. Based on that premise, it is safe to say that advertising can work in the same way, such as when it informs the consumers about another product that holds a significant advantage over the product/service currently being used.

So, what determines customer attitude resistance? It is safe to say that it all depends on how strong a foundation the attitude is built upon. Direct experience with the attitude object often leads to firmly entrenched attitudes that are to a greater extent opposed to change. A strong foundation provides a basis for resisting counter attitudinal attacks.

Feelings As Part of the Advertising Experience

In addition to understanding the feelings experienced during product and/or service consumption, it is very essential to understand the feelings experienced when customers are processing advertising messages which they have to deal with constantly. Just as the feelings experienced during consumption determine customers' post-consumption evaluations, so too do those feelings experienced during advertisement processing determine customers' post-message evaluations. Attitudes toward the advertised products/services are more favorable after viewing an advertisement which evokes positive feelings. Conversely, advertisements which elicit negative feelings can cause consumers to hold less favorable product/service attitudes. One way organizations can affect customers' attitudes is to influence how they feel during attitude formation. A new store, for example, might find it worthwhile to give shoppers a small gift when they enter the store as a way of enhancing their mood. Advertisers may find it beneficial from placing their messages in television shows which evoke positive moods while avoiding those that may depress the customers' mood states.

Attitude Resistance

Attitude resistance refers to the degree to which an attitude is immune to the prevailing changes in the global marketplace. In most cases, consumers' attitude change because people encounter something that warrants process revision. Some attitudes are highly resistant to change; others are much more malleable. Companies want their customers' product attitudes to be highly resistant. This makes them less vulnerable to competitive attacks. One indication of a company's vulnerability to competitive attacks is the resistance nature of its customers' attitudes toward its products and/or services. When consumers hold undesirable beliefs because they have misperceived the offering (e.g., consumers who overestimate product price), efforts should focus on bringing these beliefs into harmony with reality. If, however, customers are accurate in their perceptions of a product's limitations, it may be necessary to change the product itself.

Customers' resistance to change should be considered because there are a lot of alternative changes that one might consider implementing for increasing customers' liking of a certain product brand relative to its competitor. In the absence of actual product and/or service change, it is almost impossible to beliefs derived from actual consumption of any given product/service. It is very important to note that a company's vulnerability to competitive attacks is the resistance of its customers' attitudes toward its products and/or services. On the contrary, recruiting competitors' customers is much easier when doing so calls for changing the customers' attitudes, and these attitudes are less resistant to change.

The big question to ask is: What determines attitude resistance? The answer depends on how strong any given foundation the attitude is built upon. Direct experience with the attitude object often leads to firmly entrenched attitudes that are resistant to change. On the contrary, attitudes based on indirect experience, such as those formed after seeing an advertisement or hearing what someone else has to say about the attitude object, are usually more susceptible to change.

Environmental Influences on Customer Behavior

Individuals come in all shapes, sizes, and colors, and behave in a variety of ways. These characteristics are what make an individual unique. Consumers are shaped to some extent by the environment in which they live, and they in turn affect their environments through their behaviors. External influences such as culture, ethnicity, and social class influence how individual customers buy and use products/services, and help explain how consumer segments behave.

Culture

Culture is the complex of values, ideas, artifacts, and other meaningful symbols which help individuals to communicate, interpret, and evaluate members of society. Culture has also to a certain extent, been defined as a set of socially acquired behavior patterns transmitted symbolically through language and other means to the members of a particular society. Culture does not include instincts or idiosyncratic behavior occurring as a one-time solution to a unique problem. It is however, a reflection of certain influences from factors such as ethnicity, race, religion, and national or regional identity. Culture includes both abstract and material elements, which allow us to describe, evaluate, and differentiate cultures. Abstract elements include values, attitudes, idea, personality types, and summary constructs, such as religion or politics.

Additionally, material components also most commonly referred to as cultural artifacts, include such things as books, computers, tools, buildings, and things like buildings. Culture provides people with a sense of identity and an understanding of acceptable behavior within society.

As the competitive environment in the global marketplace continues to alter the way companies operate, customer service takes center stage. Companies must find new approaches of dealing with the complicated environment of multicultural diversity in order to effectively market their products to the consumers without compromising quality service. Ethnic groups may be formed around nationality, religion, physical attributes, or geographic location. In the United States, social classes are divided into six groups: 1. Upper upper; 2. Lower Upper; 3. Upper Middle; 4. Lower Middle; 5. Upper Lower; and 6. Lower Lower. Each group displays characteristic values and behaviors that are useful to consumer analysts in order to find ways and means of designing marketing programs which can help in keeping pace with the competition in the global marketplace.

Values and Norms

The two important elements of culture are values and norms. Norms are rules of behavior held by a majority or at least a consensus of a group about how individuals should behave.

On the other hand, cultural values are those values shared broadly across groups of people, whereas personal values are the goals or instrumental beliefs of individuals. There is a great difference between societal and personal values; values tend to vary among people of the same culture.

Values and norms represent the very beliefs of various groups within a society. Macroculture refers to values and symbols which apply to the entire society or to most of its citizen. Some countries, such as the United States and Switzerland, have national cultures made up of many microcultures, whereas other countries, such as Japan, tend to be more of homogeneous in nature. United States marketers must be ready to adapt to the changing needs of the global market environment as influenced by the constant changes in the diverse ethnic groups and many microcultures.

Adopting Strategies to Changing Cultures

It must be emphasized that culture is adaptive, and as such, marketing strategies based on the values of society must be adaptive. When cultural changes happen, trends develop and provide marketing opportunities to the changes based on the competitive environment in the global marketplace. As cultures evolve, marketers can associate products or brand benefits with new values, or other necessary changes deemed appropriate to counter the competitive environment in the global marketplace.

Due to the competitive environment in the global marketplace, all companies big and small are confronted with the challenge of addressing consumer socialization, the acquisition of consumption-related cognitions, attitudes, and behavior. More than often, cultural norms change easily, and sometimes they stay the same for quite a long time. Norms learned early in life may be highly resistant to promotional efforts, thereby creating s scramble among marketers who strive daily to keep pace with the marketing environment in the global marketplace. Culture has a profound effect on why and how people buy and consume products and services. Culture impacts the specific products people buy as well as the structure of consumption, individual decision making, and communication in a society.

Influence of Culture on Pre-Purchase and Purchase Proper

It is very important to note that culture impacts the need, search, and alternative evaluation stages of how individuals make purchase decisions in a variety of ways. Marketers of various products/services time and time again are confronted with the challenge of influencing the consumers in the stages through point-of-purchase displays, advertising, and retailing strategies. Cultures view differently what is needed to enjoy a good standard of living. Culture affects how consumers are likely to search for information. In some cultures, word-of-mouth and advice from a family member about a certain product/service of brand choice are more important than the information found in an advertisement. On the contrary, some cultures are more likely to search the Internet for information. Notwithstanding any given method, marketers are faced with the challenge of understanding what part is valued more in a particular culture in order to formulate the most effective information strategy.

As we continue to analyze culture, it is important to understand that culture affects how customers use or consume products and services. Products are first and foremost bought to obtain function, form, and meaning, all of which companies producing products and offering various services must address since they are defined by the cultural context of consumption. Culture influences how individuals dispose of products. Consequently, washing machines are almost a disposable product in the United States. When washing machines break down or when the customer moves, they are often left behind or discarded. Some cultures promote reselling products after use, giving them to others to use, or recycling them and their packaging when possible, whereas, others support throwing them away.

Just as customers form pre-purchase evaluations, to assist them in deciding which products/services they should purchase, they also form post-consumption evaluations about the purchased products/services. Typically, companies examine the post-purchase evaluations in terms of customer service satisfaction. Understanding customer service satisfaction is essential for a number of reasons. The level of customer satisfaction or dissatisfaction influences repeat buying, word-of-mouth communication, and complaint behavior. Additionally, an understanding of the elements of customer satisfaction or dissatisfaction of competitors' customers greatly enables a company to effectively and efficiently keep pace with the competition.

Society's values continuously change even though the core values are relatively permanent. As the trend in the global marketplace continues to shift, companies must pay special attention to values in transition because they affect the size of the market segments. Family provides the basis of dominant transfusive agent of values in most cultures such as:

(a) Less time for in-home or parent-child influence. With many mothers working outside of the home, about 65 of 4 to 6 year-olds attend preschool or day-care compared to 6.7 percent in 1965. Today, children are increasingly learning their values outside of the family from babysitters, schools, and of course, the media. The increasing in single-mother births also diminishes the potential parental influence on children.

(b) The number of divorce rates. Most children are now raised in single-parent households, contributing to decreased family influence. The children born in single-parent households are more likely to form and live in traditional families, influencing values of the future generation.

(c) The isolated nuclear family. Due to the increased mobility of jobs and education, there is geographic of the nuclear families from grandparents and other relatives, thereby contributing to the lack of heritage or roots thereof.

The Influence of Age-Related Microcultures on Values

In addition to families, and religious institutions, culture and values are shaped by early life experiences. Customer analysts must employ cohort analysis to investigate the changes in patterns of behavior or attitudes of groups called cohorts. A cohort is a group of individuals linked as a group in some way-usually by age. Cohort analysis focuses on actual changes in the behavior or attitudes of a cohort, the changes that can be attributed to the process of aging, and changes that are associated with events of a particular period, such as the Great Depression or the Watergate Scandal.

National Culture and the Impact on Consumers

Culture has a profound impact on the way customers perceive various products and/or services, purchasing processes, and the companies from which products are purchased. Companies are challenged to give more attention, however, to understanding macrocultures and how they affect customer behavior. According to Hofstede, there are four dimensions of culture that are common among 66 countries, and they are:

(a) **Individualism versus collectivism:** Individualism describes the relationship between an individual and fellow individuals, or the collectivity that prevails in society.

(b) **Uncertainty avoidance:** Uncertainty avoidance concerns the different ways in which societies react to the uncertainties and ambiguities inherent in life. Some societies require well-defined rules or rituals to guide behavior, whereas others are tolerant of deviant ideas and behavior

(c) **Power distance:** Power distance reflects the degree to which a society accepts inequality in power at different levels in organizations and institutions. Power distance can affect preferences for centralization of authority, acceptance of differential rewards, and the ways people of unequal status interact with each other.

(d) Masculinity-femininity: This dimension defines the extent to which societies hold values traditionally regarded as predominantly masculine or feminine. Assertiveness, respect for achievement, and the acquisition of money and material possessions are identified with masculinity; and nurturing, concern for environment, and championing the underdog are associated with a culture's femininity.

Social Class Microcultures

Microcultures can be described in terms of social class. Social class is defined as relatively permanent and homogeneous divisions in a society into which individuals or families sharing similar values, lifestyles, interests, wealth, status, education, economic positions, and behavior can be categorized. Social class is to a large extent influenced by the family in which individuals are raised. Variables which determine social class have been identified in social stratification studies since the early 1930s. Today, social class research includes thousands of studies dealing with the measurement of social class with gender, race, ethnicity, and education; and the effects of social class on poverty and economic policy. Social class affects the consumer behavior in a variety of ways. Customers associate brands of products and/or services with specific social classes. For example, Heineken and Amstel beers are considered to be upper middle-class drinks, whereas Budweiser is perceived to be a beer to everyone, and is typically consumed by middle- and lower-class drinkers.

Market Segmentation

Given the competitive nature in the global marketplace, social class can be used to segment markets. Following are the steps for market segmentation:

(a) Identification of social class usage of products and/or services.

(b) Comparison of social class variables for segmentation with other variables (life cycle, income, etc.,)

(c) Description of social class characteristics identified in market target.

(d) Development of marketing program to maximize effectiveness of marketing mix based on consistency with social class attributes.

Analysis of market segments by socioeconomic profile helps in the development of a comprehensive marketing process to match the preferences and behavior of the market segment. Targeting various zip codes facilitates social class segmentation.

Zip codes estimate status without the need for collecting additional data from respondents other than addresses.

Social class is an essential concept in developing positioning strategies-the creation of perceptions in consumers' minds about the attributes of a product and/or services of any given organization. To accomplish positioning effectively calls for a good understanding of the class characteristics of the target market and the class attributes desired for the products and/ or services.

The Important Characteristics of Customer Service

Customer service possesses several unique characteristics that often have a significant impact on customer service program development. With the competition in the global marketplace continuing to change on a daily basis, these special features of customer service may cause unique problems and result in customer service decisions that are substantially different from those found in other business operation segments. Some of the more important of the customer service characteristics are: Intangibility; Inseparability; perishability and fluctuating demand; A client relationship; Customer effort; and Uniformity.

Intangibility

It is safe to say that the basic difference between goods and services is the intangibility of services, and many of the problems encountered while rendering and marketing those services due to their intangibility nature. As the competition in the global marketplace continues to change, companies are confronted with the challenge of dealing with how quality, in most cases, exceptional quality service, is being managed. Because many services cannot appeal to a buyer's touch, taste, smell, sight, or hearing before purchase, puts a greater challenge on companies to re-evaluate how they approach how services are offered to customers of all needs.

Depending on the type of services being offered, the intangibility factor often dictates use of direct channels due to the need for personal contact between buyers and sellers.

Inseparability

It is very essential to note that services cannot be separated from the person of the seller. To put it the other way, the services must be produced and marketed simultaneously. Based on the simultaneous production and marketing nature of most services, the main concern is the creation of time and place utility. For example, a bank teller produces the services of receiving deposits and markets other appropriate bank services at the same time. Many services, therefore, are tailored and not mass produced.

The implication of customer service inseparability is very important to note. Inseparable services cannot be inventoried, and thus direct sale is the only feasible channel of distribution. The quality of customer service is sometimes not easy to standardize due to the inability to completely mechanize the service encounter. However, some companies, through technology innovation, are able to overcome or, at least, alleviate challenges associated with the inseparability characteristics of customer service. In addition to the technological innovation, tangible representation of service can serve to overcome the inseparability problem. For example, in the insurance industry, a contract serves as the tangible representation of the services offered. The service itself remains inseparable from the seller (insurance provider), but the buyer has a tangible representation of the service in the form of an insurance policy. This enables the use of intermediaries (agents) in the marketing of insurance.

Perishability and Fluctuating Demand

Services are perishable and markets for most services fluctuate either by season, days, or time of day. Unused telephone capacity and electrical power; vacant seats on planes, trains, buses, and stadiums; and time spent by catalog services representatives waiting for customers to reach them all represent business that is lost for good. The combination of perishability and fluctuating demand presents a variety of problems as far as customer service is concerned. Specifically, in the areas of staffing and distribution, there is a great need to provide exceptional customer service that are geared toward meeting the needs of the consumers.

Client Relationship

The competitive environment in the global marketplace has changed the way services are provided to customer segments in every business industry. It is therefore, very important to note that in the marketing of a great many services, a customer relationship exists between the buyer and the seller. In other words, the buyer views the seller as someone who has knowledge that is of value. Examples of this type of relationship are the physician-patient, college-professor-student, and accountant-small business owner. The buyer, to a large extent, abides by the advice or suggestions offered by the seller, and this relationship is ongoing in nature.

Customer Effort

To a great degree, customers are involved in the production many types of service. In some restaurants, customers clean their tables. Customers sometimes carry their luggages to carts packed next to a baggage compartment of the plane. If an organization purchases the services of an advertising agency, employees will have to work with the agency, review its ideas, and find new innovative ways to improve customer service. Every operations has varying degrees of rendering services to the customers.

Uniformity

The quality of service can vary more than the quality of goods. Producers of goods have producers to prevent, identify, and correct defects. Because services are offered by humans, it is very important to note that in the process, services are customized to the needs of customers, hence the need to offer quality service.

In today's increasingly competitive environment, quality service is one of the critical components of competing effectively in the global marketplace. Unlike products in which quality is often measured against standards, service quality is measured against performance. Since customer service is frequently produced in the presence of a customer, is labor intensive, and is not able to be stored or objectively examined, the definition of what constitutes good quality of customer service may be difficult. Customers determine the value of service quality in relation to available alternatives and their particular needs.

The Importance of Customer Service as a tool to Competitive Environment the Marketplace.

Customer service can make or break your business. If people find your employees are rude or don't know what they're talking about they'll go elsewhere to make their purchases. You don't want that, so it's important to train them on good customer service and then monitor it so they continue to do a job with it. When customer service is high customer satisfaction will be even higher and that's perfect for business.

Customer service can be in many forms and you may not even realize you're doing it, so you must pay attention and know what you're doing at all times. For example, if a customer walks through your door and says, do you have this product? If you don't, but you have one that'll do the same thing, you need to say, I'm sorry we don't, but we do have this product and it'll serve the same purpose. That's customer service.

Customer service can also be used on the phone. No matter what type of business you run, customers call on the phone. They may want to know your hours of operation or they may have a question about a purchase they recently made. No matter what the reason is for the call it's important that the person answering the phone knows how to do it properly and is kind at all times. People will continue to do business with you if they're treated fairly and with respect. Rude and inconsiderate people will drive people away faster than anything else.

Following up with customers is another form of customer service. When you show your customers you care about them and you want to make sure they have everything they need and that the products are working properly, they'll remember that. They won't be afraid to come to you when there's a problem and they won't think twice about recommending you to their friends and family.

One last form of customer service you need to make sure happens is helping your customers. No matter if they're young or old; helping them to the car when they have an arm load of products is a good way to show them you care. Helping them decide on which products to purchase and helping them to understand which ones will work well together is another way.

It's important to remember your customers are what will keep you in business. If they're not happy they'll leave and go to your competition. When you have good customer service each and every time a customer comes through the door they'll be happy to come back to you and they'll invite their friends and family as well.

Customer Service Satisfaction Measurement

Customer quality service and satisfaction are of growing concern to all businesses throughout the world, and research of the customer service topics generally focus on two issues: (1) Understanding the expectations and requirements of the customers, and (2) Determining how well companies and their major competitors are succeeding in satisfying customers' expectations and requirements. Customers determine the value of service quality in relation to available alternatives and their particular needs. Problems in the determination of quality customer service are attributable to differences in the expectations, perceptions, and experiences regarding the encounter between the service provider and consumers. Excellent customer service is achieved by providing an enjoyable experience for customers. This is done by listening to customers and determining their needs and desires. Anticipating the needs of customers also creates a great customer service experience. Repeat customer process is crucial for the success of any business, and losing customers is considered a reliable measure of failure since without customers there can be no business. Keeping customers satisfied also means that they are likely to bring more customers to a business by word of mouth or verbal referral, especially if their loyalty is rewarded with discounts and free gifts. One of the key ways to keep customers loyal and satisfied is to listen to them and respond to their demands.

In essence, the customer perceives the level of the service quality as being a function of the magnitude and direction of the gap between expected service and perceived service. Management of a company may not realize that they are delivering poor-quality service due to differences in the way managers and customers view acceptable quality levels. To overcome problems like this and avoid losing customers, companies must be aware of the determinants of service quality. Following are a few of the determinants of customer quality service:

(a) **Tangibles:** This category includes the physical evidence of the service. For instance, employees are always visible in a hotel lobby dusting, emptying ash trays, or otherwise cleaning up. Likewise, clean, shiny, up-to-date medical equipment are examples of tangible elements determining the customer quality service.

(b) **Reliability:** This category involves the consistency and dependability of the service performance. For instance, does the phone company or a bank always send out accurate customer statements? Likewise, does the plumber always fix the problem on the first visit?

(c) Responsiveness: This category involves the willingness or readiness of company associates to provide service to any customer. For instance, will a physician see patients on the same day they call in to say they are sick? Will the college professor who is teaching a course online, return the students' call the same day?

(d) Assurance: This category refers to the competence and knowledge of service providers and the ability to convey trust and confidence. This determinant encompasses the provider's name and reputation; possession of the necessary skills; and trustworthiness, believability, and honesty. For example, a bank will guarantee same-day loan processing; a doctor is highly trained in a particular specialty.

(e) Empathy: This category refers to the service provider's efforts to understand the consumers' needs and then provide, as best as possible, individualized quality service experience. For instance, on an airplane, flight attendants learn what type of beverages the customer may want to drink and what magazines the customers regularly read. It is very important to note that each of the above determinants plays an important role in how the customer views the quality of service offered by the companies. Converting the quality of service into a powerful competitive weapon calls for continuously striving for service superiority-consistently performing above and beyond the adequate service level and capitalizing on opportunities for exceeding the desired level of service.

Despite traditional thinking and practices on the part of many company managers and writers concerning the similarities between the operation of manufacturing and services organizations, the past decade has experienced the growth of many innovative ways of meeting customer service challenges. The customer service challenges are the quest to (a) constantly develop new quality services that will meet or exceed customers' needs, (b) improve on the quality and variety of existing services, and (c) provide and distribute these services in a manner that best serves the needs of the customer.

So What Determines Customer Satisfaction?

It is very important to note that a critical determinant of customer satisfaction is based on the consumers' perceptions of the product's performance during its consumption. Poor performance and unfavorable product/service consumption experiences usually guarantee that customers will be dissatisfied with the products/services unless there are extenuating circumstances. Generally, the more favorable the products/services' performance, the greater the customers' satisfaction.

Companies that are successful in satisfying their customers' needs often find it advantageous to advertise this success. Doing so reinforces the attitudes of current customers. It also enhance the pre-purchase evaluations of consumers whom the companies wish to recruit. One example of such advertising appears in Figure 1.4. This ad informs the customers that it is ranked number one in customer satisfaction. This ranking is based on a survey conducted by J.D. Powers and Associates, a market research firm that built its reputation on measuring customer satisfaction.

Beyond influencing customer satisfaction through its impact on confirmation or dissatisfaction, expectations may directly affect satisfaction. This is due to the fact that expectations may color or bias the interpretation of the consumption experience itself. Expectations do not always bias post-consumption evaluations. It depends on the ambiguity of the consumption experience. Can customers truly determine whether they are benefitting from taking vitamins? How do we know whether the person who repaired the car or TV took advantage of the situation by unnecessarily replacing parts that were in working condition? It turns out that for many consumption experiences, it is virtually impossible for customers to determine whether the product/service performs as expected. And in these instances, post-consumption evaluations may be particularly susceptible to initial expectations. On the contrary, unambiguous consumption experiences provide better grounds for evaluating the consumed item, thereby reducing the opportunity for expectations to affect evaluations directly.

Attracting consumers to patronize different business establishments includes performing well on the attributes which customers think are most important-location, nature and quality of assortments, price, advertising and promotion, sales personnel, services offered, physical attributes, store clientele, store atmosphere, and post-transaction services. Customer service is not a jigsaw puzzle and neither is it a special department. Customer service philosophy is what every business should practice, no matter how big or small it is. Customer service can be further broken down into four basic components. Whilst volumes of books are actually written about excellent service, these 4 factors may be regarded as the beginning point – the basic principles. By understanding these extremely easy ideas, you will be able to manage your customer service approach better and create magic for the clients.

4 Fundamental Aspects of a Great Customer Service Philosophy :

1. **Using common sense-** This suggests performing things that seem apparent. Hence this practice is all

about taking care of your clients just like they want to be treated. Understand that what you'd anticipate might be different from what your consumer maybe looking for. For example, a bellman might work in a really costly hotel. He'll most likely by no means stay at a resort such as the five Star in which he functions. But he very well knows what the hotel guests demand, and successfully delivers it for them.

2. **Flexibility** – Policies and Guidelines are practically nothing more than mere rules. Don't allow "business policy" stand amidst the happiness of your client. There can be a point wherein you will have to stick to these policies but customers come first in most cases. So, if they are in any way wrong, then let them stay that way with dignity. Do whatever you can do to make your consumer happy. Along with empowering individuals to become flexible there is also a major initiative of proper training. If correctly educated and the workers are trained properly then they can satisfy the customer and at the same time bring profit to the company.

3. **Solving Issues** – You'll find two kinds of issues to solve – non-business and business issues. Business issues involve taking care of complaints and meeting the customer requirements. Customers often come up with complaints, so you have to help them. Then you'll

find non – business issues that are very different from the first category. Solving non – business issues involve excellent PR skills.

4. **Recovery** – This can be among the most significant factors. You'll be able to possess a happy consumer for a long time if you have a great recovery approach. Bear in mind, research have confirmed it is a lot less expensive to keep an old customer then to have a new one. Do everything you can so as to recover from a difficult issue, and also give the customer a fresh ray of confidence why he or she should stick to your business post the recovery. This means that you need to work on a problem from all perspectives beyond just fixing it. In order to get a client back, the business has to offer some complimentary services or products that will attract the client and make him or her stay.

There you've got 4 fundamental aspects of a great customer service philosophy. These easy but potent tools will help you achieve the best of customer service results

Excellent customer service requires effective listening and communication skills. A company's customer service representatives should listen carefully to what the customer needs. The answer or solution to the problem or question should accurately address the nature of the call. Moreover, excellent communication skills are crucial. A customer should be able to easily understand what the customer service representative is saying. The representative must speak distinctly, and use common terminology that everyone understands, not highly technical language.

The customer chain

The relationship between internal customers and external customers is what forms the customer chain. If you have a back room kind of job where you rarely see the light of day, let alone a living, breathing customer, you can easily begin to feel that your work has little or no impact on external customers. But if you look at the bigger picture, you can see that everyone in a company plays some part in fulfilling the customers' needs. Barely an hour goes by during the day when you are not, in some form or another, providing something for somebody. Each interaction with an internal customer is an important link in a chain of events that always ends up at the external customers' feet.

By addressing less obvious customer needs such as listening with empathy to customers when they have a problem or providing options and alternatives when you can't give customers exactly what they want, you widen the gap between you and your competitors. Good or bad, customer service leaves an indelible impression on potential and existing customers, even in today's fast paced, technological environment. And truth be told, most folks will endure more, pay more, and show fierce loyalty for courteous treatment, small perks, and the feeling of being valued. Whether it's a liberal "return policy" at a store, businesses that acknowledge and reward your "relationship anniversary" with them, or service with a smile.

In conclusion, it must be emphasized that ccustomer service that exceeds expectations gives customers a sense of satisfaction and creates a feeling of goodwill towards an organization. This encourages them to develop positive perceptions and to return, i.e. creating customer loyalty. Customers start to develop trust and confidence in the Brands.

www.ingramcontent.com/pod-product-compliance
Lightning Source LLC
Chambersburg PA
CBHW021049180526
45163CB00005B/2355